Copyright © 2012

www.CEORealTalk.com

All rights reserved. No part of this book may be reproduced in any form, except for the inclusion of brief quotations to review, without permission in writing from the author/publisher.

The authors and SkillBites make no representation or warranties with respect to the accuracy, applicability, fitness, or completeness of the contents of this course. They disclaim all warranties (expressed or implied), merchantability, or fitness for any particular purpose. The author and SkillBites shall in no event be held liable for any loss or other damages, including but not limited to special, incidental, consequential, or other damages.

This book is licensed for your personal enjoyment only. If you would like to share this book with another person, please purchase an additional copy for each recipient. Thank you for respecting the hard work of this author.

Acknowledgements

We want to express our appreciation to Odette Moore for designing the cover for our book and to our husbands, Eric Newcombe and Keith Dixson, and family for their ongoing support.

ISBN-10: 1493584359

ISBN-13: 978-1493584352

Table of Contents

Introduction 3
Strengthening Your Business 4
Growing Your Business 8
Leading Your Business 13
Enjoying Your Business 16
Summary 19
Additional Resources 20
Action Plan 22
About the Authors 23
Testimonials 25

Introduction

As a small business owner or entrepreneur, there are many obvious things that are clamoring for your attention: get clients, do the work, pay the bills, etc. However, what about, the less obvious? From being in business for over 25 years combined, we believe that it is vital to get past the obvious and address the hidden nuances, problems, and attitudes that can derail you – whether you've been in business for 1 month, 1 year, or 10 years.

This book will increase your awareness in four key areas of business development, giving you a realistic foundation to promote long-term profitability. We know the power of these "less than obvious" issues, because we have been through them all – and have come out the other side with our businesses stronger than ever.

It's time for real talk about real issues – so you can discover real solutions.

Strengthening Your Business

5 Hidden Nuances that can Destroy Your Business

The statistics are sobering: only 49% of new businesses last five years or more, and only 34% last 10 years or more.[1]

Why the heavy attrition rate? Many experts have addressed various reasons businesses fail, citing inadequate cash flow, high overhead costs, bad management practices, poor credit, and too-rapid expansion as key factors. However, in our many years as seasoned entrepreneurs, we have identified five less-obvious factors that can completely destroy a business if gone unaddressed. These are particularly critical when just starting out, but they can spell disaster for a business at any time.

1. Not Being 100% Committed

In the early years of starting a company, most business owners feel stretched financially. Many combat this by developing a contingency plan: they either work at night or on weekends at another job just in case their business fails. However, by straddling the fence, you are tacitly giving yourself the option to fail. The "hidden nuance" here, which could have destroyed both our businesses, is that if you are putting time and effort into a back-up plan, you cannot make a full commitment to your business.

When you decide that failure is *not* an option and acknowledge that the livelihood of your family depends

---

[1] Source: U.S. Dept. of Commerce, Census Bureau, Business Dynamics Statistics; U.S. Dept. of Labor, Bureau of Labor Statistics, BED.

solely on your business, you will give it your 100% commitment – and will consequently have a greater chance at success.

2. Not Understanding Your Financials

Not understanding your financials – that is, not knowing what's coming in and what's going out of your company – is another "hidden nuance" that puts your business at high risk for failure. Of course, operating blind is not something most business owners want to admit to. We certainly didn't.

When we started our businesses, our number one goal was to ensure that our staff had what they required to operate efficiently and effectively. It seemed like a good, strategic goal – until we realized that we had enough office supplies, office equipment, and extra materials to open up a second-hand supply store each. And – of even greater importance – we had to close down projects and locations due to lack of funds. We realized that we were not in control of our businesses because we didn't have a clue as to how, why, and when our staff made purchases.

The bottom line is that you need to understand your **revenue** bottom line – and all the other lines in your financials. Know what you're spending and where you can cut back. Establish systems and processes to control purchasing and inventory. Set up budgets for projects and ensure that they are followed.

It's important that you not only *generate* financial reports, but that you *understand* them. It is *your* responsibility to watch over business finances: not the accountant's, the bookkeeper's, or the division manager's. Not knowing your financials will quickly position your business to fail.

3. Not Focusing on Your Business Opportunity

"I want to help." "I've always dreamed of owning my own business." "I love what I do." These are often sound bites that business owners share with the world. Unfortunately, the "I" mindset is a "hidden nuance" that will keep a business from succeeding.

What we have learned over the years is that the foundation of a good business is not an emotion or a dream or a sense of satisfaction. Those are nice, but they are not sufficient to build a solid and successful business. The foundation of a good business is *a good business opportunity*. The number one focus for any business owner should be to fulfill a need in the marketplace. It's not about *your* dream or fulfilling *your* interest, but about whether people want, need, and are willing to pay for your product or service.

4. Not Being Prepared for Economic Downturns

As business owners, we dare to dream about saving money or building a cushion for a rainy day. However, we often have the mindset that we are barely getting by and, consequently, saving doesn't happen. Because of this attitude and approach, many businesses were forced to close their doors, or came very near to it, during the economic downturn from 2008-2011. Not being prepared for an economic downturn is a "hidden nuance" that can be devastating.

Whether or not you are in a position to put money aside as a cushion, you can prepare for an economic downturn by staying abreast of your customers' buying trends, identifying those customers who may be entering the "slow pay" zone (70- to 90-day payments), restructuring staff duties to increase productivity, and cutting back on unnecessary spending.

5. Not Following Up for Repeat Business

Sometimes businesses take their customers for granted. We've all done it! Once we obtain our customers' business, we don't follow up or ask, "How are we doing?" Moreover, we fail to ask, "Is there anything we can do better?"

Not following up is a "hidden nuance" that leads to losing repeat business. Sales decrease, and customer complaints increase. By the time you reach that point, it is often too late. Avoid the possibility of losing business by taking the time to recognize your customers, solicit their feedback, and ask them how you can do better.

Growing Your Business

5 Essential Strategies for Hiring the Best Workforce

Several studies reveal that the single greatest challenge for human resource staff working in medium to large businesses is the inability to recruit and retain good employees and managers. Small businesses have an even greater challenge because most lack the funding necessary to purchase state-of-the-art software that can automatically search and screen resumes, and streamline the interviewing process.

The good news is that by getting past the obvious, small businesses can attract and retain qualified employees to create an elite workforce – without making a significant monetary investment. The five strategies below simply require a different way of approaching and implementing the hiring process.

1. Adopt a Companywide Commitment to Candidates

The employees we hire are considered "high profile" individuals: they engage directly with our customers. They are our businesses' most important asset. With that in mind, we determined years ago that the entire hiring process should *assist* rather than *deter* job candidates if we were really serious about attracting top-notch employees.

We encourage you to do the same, by championing a companywide commitment to your future employees. This commitment translates into a hiring process that includes:

- Clear, understandable job announcements and instructions for applying.

- Timely and informed responses to questions about the requirements and the process.

- A user-friendly application process that is not overwhelming or burdensome.

- Scheduled follow-ups or acknowledgements that an application has been received.

- The invitation for job applicants to check in for updates on the status of their applications during a specific time of the day as decisions are reached.

2. Leverage Job Applications for Evaluating Candidates

A second essential strategy for small business owners to implement is the use of an application in addition to a résumé. An application is a screening device: it serves as a preliminary evaluation of a candidate's abilities. It provides a simple test of the applicant's ability to spell, write, give factual answers to questions, and pay attention to simple details. It also becomes part of the permanent employee record as a legal document. The immediate benefit to small businesses is that candidates who take the time to fill out an application are more likely to be really interested in the position and will consequently provide truthful and useful information. What is also significant is that an application protects a business owner in the case of falsification on the part of the employee, which can be grounds for dismissal.

3. Move Away from Traditional Job Descriptions

Another essential strategy we use to obtain the best workforce is to create a "role profile" for each open position instead of the traditional job description. The term "role profile" has been around for years: it indicates a blend of the job description (i.e., responsibilities and key deliverables for the job) and personal qualities (i.e., knowledge, skills, and behaviors necessary to perform the job well). The result is a complete "profile" of the type of person who would best fit the role.

A role profile simultaneously provides job candidates with a clear and concise picture of the job and decreases the company's cost for recruitment and retention by effectively matching qualified candidates with the open position. Moreover, using a role profile allows the selected candidate to know and understand expected outcomes and what it takes to be successful in the position. Since the implementation of this strategy, both our companies have experienced an increase in top-talent candidates responding to our open positions nationwide.

4. Incorporate a Pre-Hire Job Demonstration

A résumé, an application, references, and even a personal interview can only take you so far. You want to know for a fact that the job applicant possesses the skillset and abilities necessary to perform the job requirements at the time of hire. A pre-hire job demonstration can accomplish exactly that.

We developed a demonstration exercise several years ago that has proven to be a practical and efficient way to determine whether a job applicant has the necessary skills prior to hire:

- The job applicant is given a role profile questionnaire to fill out prior to the interview or upon completing the employment application.

- The job applicant is asked to either role play or perform the actual job for 30 minutes (whichever is appropriate to the position).

- After the job demonstration, the candidate is provided with five questions about the job and is asked to respond in an essay format and submit their answers the following day.

The job demonstration and essay responses can then be combined with the résumé, application, references, and interview in a comprehensive evaluation.

5. Hire from within the Community

Our final essential strategy is to hire a workforce that mirrors the community in which it operates. This can be done by networking with and using local workforce center referral programs, and by asking employees, vendors, and clients for recommendations to find top talent.

Since implementing this strategy over 14 years ago, both our companies have become well known in our respective communities and we are ranked among the best places to work. Our corporate cultures, business leadership styles, and local outreach efforts reflect our companies' persistent commitment to put people to work in our community. By advocating this approach, we increase our community's economic base, create a more inclusive workforce, and foster an environment where every person can live, work, and shop in their own community.

Leading Your Business

5 CEO Decision-Making Pitfalls to Avoid

As CEOs of small businesses, we have total responsibility for every aspect of our companies. When we first started our businesses, we did everything. That meant running the day-to-day operations, hiring personnel, paying bills, marketing, seeking funding, and even deciding what type of furniture would be placed in the office. Unsurprisingly, our first approach to leading our staff was simply to have them follow instructions correctly; input or feedback wasn't expected or requested.

However, as our businesses grew, we needed to get past the obvious objective of "get the job done" to the more important goal of "get the job done right." The fact was, the burden of our responsibilities and our desire to control risk were creating unhealthy behaviors that were sabotaging our businesses. We identified five highly dysfunctional decision-making behaviors that all small business owners should be aware of – and avoid!

1. Controlling Mode

As a small business owner, the future of your business will often flash before your eyes without warning. With that stark mental picture in mind, it is natural to resist relinquishing control or delegating tasks – to believe that "I am the only one who can get things done quickly and efficiently." But in reality, this dysfunctional behavior will hinder rather than help, since it does not permit you to focus on the areas of the business that truly require your personal attention and effort.

www.skillbites.net

2. Paralysis Mode

Not making a decision is equal to making a bad decision, if not worse. It is easy as a small business owner to want a complete analysis of a situation and full information before deciding what to do. But many times, that is not realistic and this "wait-and-see" attitude delays decisions unnecessarily. It is better to take the available information, couple it with your CEO intuition or "gut feeling," and make a great decision.

3. Obstruction Mode

Unconsciously, as business owners, we develop long and drawn out approval processes to weigh the pros and cons of the simplest decisions. This type of deferment is usually rooted in our fear of making mistakes and failing. However, this behavior stifles our employees' ability to be proactive and forward thinking, and denies them the ability to assume full responsibility for what they are being paid to do. The end result is that employees disengage and do not feel accountable for the business's overall productivity. A slow decision-making process and constant waiting cause unnecessary delays when the decision could have been made quickly by the staff member in charge.

4. Distrust Mode

In "distrust mode," we hire employees, pay them, and then do their job for them! Not allowing employees to take ownership in their area of expertise and preventing them from making decisions is an unhealthy behavior and exhibits distrust. You need to make the decision to trust your employees: it is a huge step, but a necessary one if your goal is to grow and expand your services.

5. Penny-wise Mode

As CEOs, we initially found the cost, time, and effort involved in training our employees to be a challenge and a struggle. But we soon realized that not investing in our employees was "penny-wise and pound-foolish" – the benefits of training far outweighed the expense!

Training is essential if you want to maintain a well-qualified team. Finding money and time to train will increase your business opportunities as your employees will have a rich understanding of your company's mission, vision, and decision-making process. The end result is a positive work environment where responsible and accountable decision-making is valued and appreciated at all levels.

Enjoying Your Business

5 Techniques to Create True Work-Life Balance

The era we live in today is difficult and requires us to prioritize and balance our work and family life. We firmly believe that if we get past the obvious "work non-stop and eventually everything will come right" attitude, we can achieve a true, healthy work-life balance. It may not be perfect (what is, in life?), but it will be a happy medium full of joy and satisfaction. Here are five techniques that can help you get there.

1. Recognize the Role of Work

Work plays a significant part in life. Hard work keeps the lights on, pays the mortgage, makes the car payment, funds retirement, and permits yearly vacations. As small business owners, adopting the right mindset allows us to celebrate and enjoy the fruits of our labor.

2. Know and Own Your Support System

When we started our businesses, we had a huge network of support. However, over time, much of that support system dwindled away. People tend to move on or just plain disappear due to no fault on anybody's part. But there were certain family members and friends who remained constant and never wavered. You need to know and own a core support group as well.

The people in your support system will help you remain on target and energize you: they become a driving force for your business success. Your support system will ground you through good times and bad. They will help you stay mentally and physically healthy by reminding you to carve out family time, exercise time, and laughter time. This, in turn, will generate an overall sense of well-being for you.

3. Develop a Schedule for Work and Family

A schedule is a good thing – it keeps you accountable, to both work and family. For ourselves, we schedule meetings from 6:00 a.m. to 8:00 a.m. daily to work and discuss business goals for CEO Real Talk. This allows us to be available for our individual businesses during the work day, and to establish a cut-off time to be with our family. Develop a schedule that works for you and stick with it to create a true work-life balance.

4. Learn to Breathe

As a small business owner, work can get so fast-paced that you practically hyperventilate. Alternatively, when you are making important decisions, you might find yourself literally or figuratively holding your breath. Neither state can be maintained for long if you want to be healthy. Relax. Release. Breathe.

As you slow down and learn to breathe, it gives you the opportunity to regroup and assess where you are. It permits you to select a productive mindset and make appropriate decisions on what needs to happen next. Is learning to deal with stress challenging? Yes. For instance, we had to create a "yes/no" list for work we would accept or turn down, and stick with it. We also had to make a conscious decision to shut down our business mindset each day at a certain time and plug into family 100%. The process of breathing teaches us a lot about the process of letting go.

5. Be Present, Consistent, and Accountable

As business owners, being present requires us to be attentive at home, at work, and during "free" time. The quality of being present makes a significant and positive impact on our surroundings. Being consistent requires us to realize that what we do each and every day matters. Where we spend our time and energy has a direct connection to how successful we are. Finally, being accountable allows amazing and wonderful things to happen. For us, work-life balance is a necessity to being successful in growing our businesses.

Summary

Key Points to Remember:

1. Strengthen your business by recognizing and understanding the hidden nuances in this book.

2. Review, adopt and apply the 5 essential strategies for hiring the best workforce.

3. Understand and avoid the 5 highly dysfunctional decision-making behaviors in this book.

4. Practice and apply the 5 techniques that will create a true work-life balance.

Additional Resources

CEOReal Talk Business Mentoring Service – As part of our initiative to help, we have developed an alternative avenue for entrepreneurs to follow in the mind-set path of seasoned entrepreneurs and wise colleagues who can share knowledge, experience and open doors to otherwise out-of-reach business growth opportunities via our one-to-one business mentoring services. Visit the CEO Real Talk website at www.ceorealtalk.com and click on Business Mentoring Services.

Small Business Administration – The help Newcombe's company, HPC, received from the Los Angeles Small Business Administration District Office continued beyond the educational sessions and 8(a) certification process. The assigned Business Development Specialist in the Los Angeles District Office continues to work closely with HPC to match contracting opportunities. Our strong partnership and the individualized attention the Los Angeles District Office provides to small businesses have allowed HPC to grow and provide excellent job opportunities and has aided in HPC's overall mission of providing economic development nationwide. Website: www.SBA.gov

Count Me In for Women's Economic Independence – the leading national not-for-profit provider of resources, business education and community support for women entrepreneurs seeking to grow micro-businesses into million dollar enterprises. Count Me In has inspired us to take control of the potential of success by providing a wealth of virtual tools and resources, and a variety of peer exchange platforms all designed to help women business owners substantially and sustainably increase revenues and create new jobs. Website: http://countmein.org/

Women Impacting Public Policy (WIPP) – The Voice for Women in Business in our Nation's Capital, Women Impacting Public Policy, Inc. WIPP educates women business owners on economic policy and current legislative initiatives that impact business health and growth. Website: http://www.wipp.org/

Action Plan

Identify what actions you plan to take as a result of reading this book:

_____

_____

_____

_____

_____

_____

_____

_____

_____

_____

_____

_____

About the Authors

Garnett Newcombe is the Co-Founder and CEO of Human Potential Consultants, LLC, an award-winning employment solutions company. Established in 1997, Human Potential Consultants was founded on the belief that helping individuals improve their self-worth, work readiness, and employability skills – regardless of their background – will increase job opportunities.

Kay Woods is the Founder and CEO of Precious Treasures Childcare, an award-winning 24-hour, 7-day-a-week child care center. Established in 2002, the vision of her child care center is to strengthen family unity at the root by integrating early childhood education and parenting resources.

"We developed CEO Real Talk as an extension of our own companies to deliver effective strategies to fellow business people, based on more than 25 years of professional experience. Through CEO Real Talk, we are revealing dangerous caveats (hidden nuances) that can potentially destroy small and minority-owned businesses. It is our goal to help business owners promote realistic long-term profitability as they continue to grow and diversify." – Garnett Newcombe and Kay Woods

Other titles by Garnett Newcombe at SkillBites.net:

Be a Successful Government Contractor
Essential Strategies for Women-Owned Businesses to Take On the Government as a Customer
(http://skillbites.net/be-a-successful-government-contractor/)

Connect with Garnett Newcombe and Kay Woods

CEO Real Talk, LLC

Office: 1212 Ashby Avenue Ste A, Berkeley, CA 94702

Office #: 510-524-3497

Website: www.ceorealtalk.com
e-Mail: gnewcombe@ceorealtalk.com
e-Mail: kwoods@ceorealtalk.com
Facebook: www.facebook.com/ceorealtalk
LinkedIn: www.linkedin.com/in/ceorealtalk
Twitter: @ceorealtalk https://twitter.com/CEORealTalk

We would like to hear your feedback. Please send us your testimonial TODAY!!!

1. Has our book revealed any of the less obvious?
2. Are we on point with our tips and solutions?
3. Will you purchase or refer this book to a friend, colleague and organization?
4. Would you attend a CEO Real Talk event?
5. Are you interested in CEO Real Talk's Mentoring Program?
6. Is there anything we can do better?

Testimonials

What an amazing book I found it to be. The book was a quick read, clear and easy to follow. Having been a business owner, I could definitely relate to the nuances that we all fall prey to when running a business. I saw myself repeatedly in the book from not understanding my finances to working in the business instead of on the business. I would highly recommend this book to my colleagues who have stepped into the world of entrepreneurship. Thanks for your insight and candidness.
Joyce Redd, Employment Manager, Alameda County Behavioral Vocational Program, Alameda CA

The saying "Good things come in small packages" is the first thing that came to mind after reading *Get Past the Obvious*! This book has great insight on what is needed not only for business proprietors, but also for directors and managers in the day-to-day operations of an organization. Its strategies surrounding "work-life balance" will now hang over my desk. Thanks, Garnett and Kay, for the invaluable information.
A. Renee Daniels, TPMG Service Manager East Bay Area, Oakland, CA

www.ingramcontent.com/pod-product-compliance
Lightning Source LLC
Chambersburg PA
CBHW070737180526
45167CB00004B/1784